What the CHURCH FATHERS *say about* MARRIAGE

What the CHURCH FATHERS say about MARRIAGE

ST SHENOUDA PRESS
SYDNEY, AUSTRALIA
2025

What the Church Fathers Say about Marriage

COPYRIGHT ©2025
St. Shenouda Press

All rights reserved. Except for brief quotations in critical publications or reviews, no part of this book may be reproduced in any manner without prior written permission from the publisher.

ST SHENOUDA PRESS
8419 Putty Rd,
Putty, NSW, 2330
Sydney, Australia

www.stshenoudapress.com

ISBN 13: 978-1-7638415-1-2

TABLE OF CONTENTS

Chapter 1: The Sacred Mystery of Marriage   1

Chapter 2: Mutual Duties and Respect in Marriage   21

Chapter 3: God-Centered Marriage   41

Chapter 4: The Divine Duty of Christian Parenting   71

Chapter 1

THE SACRED MYSTERY OF MARRIAGE

St John Chrysostom
Homily 12 (Colossians 4:18)

"Epaphras, one of you and a servant of Christ, sends his greetings. He's always praying hard for you, hoping that you'll stand strong, perfect in what God wants. I can vouch for him – he really cares a lot about you, and also the people in Laodicea and Hierapolis." Colossians 4:12-13

At the start of the letter, the writer showcases a man's deep love. Love is shown not just in words of praise but also in action. It's like what he said at the beginning: 'He told us about your love in the spirit.' (Colossians 1:8) Love is demonstrated by caring deeply for someone and praying for them.

By introducing this man, he sets the stage for his words. It's important to respect a teacher because they can help students grow. And when he says, 'One of you,' it's like he's saying they should be proud of this man because they have such great people among them. He says the man is 'always fighting for you in his prayers.' He didn't just say 'praying,' but 'fighting' — like he's really worried and concerned. He vouches for him, saying, 'I can promise you, he's super passionate about you.' He's a trustworthy witness.

He emphasises again how passionate this man is about them. This means he really loves you guys and is deeply passionate about you. And also the people in Laodicea and Hierapolis. He's vouching for him to them as well.

But how would they know this? Probably they'd hear about it, but they'd also learn from reading the letter. Because he says, 'Make sure it's read in the church of the Laodiceans.' (Colossians 4:16) He wants you all to stand strong and be perfect. While this might sound like he's pointing out their flaws, he's also gently encouraging and advising them.

Some can be perfect but not stable, like if they know everything but are still shaky in their beliefs. Others might not be perfect but are stable, like if they know just a part but stand firm in it. But he wishes both for them: to stand firm and be perfect.

Notice how he reminds them about angels and the way of life. And to be filled with God's will. Because it's not enough to just do God's will. If you're truly filled, there's no room for any other desire, because you're totally convinced.

He testifies about him, saying, he has a great zeal for you. And zeal, and a lot of it, intensifying both. Just like he wrote to the Corinthians, 'I am zealous for you with a godly zeal.' (2 Corinthians 11:2) Luke, the beloved doctor, sends his greetings. This is the Gospel writer. Not putting him down by mentioning him later, but rather he's lifting up Epaphras. It's likely there are others with the same name. And also Demas.

After saying, 'Luke, the doctor, sends his greetings,' he added, 'the beloved.' Being beloved by Paul is no small compliment. It's a huge one. Greet the brothers in Laodicea, Nympha, and the church that meets at her house. See how he connects them, not just by sending greetings but also by exchanging letters.

Then again, he gives special mention, referring to him personally. He does this not casually but to inspire others to feel the same zeal. It's no small thing when he's not counted among the others. Notice how he highlights how important this man is, especially since his house was a meeting place for the church.

3

And when you guys read this letter, make sure it's also read in the church of the Laodiceans. I think there's something written there that you should hear too. It's often more helpful for them when they recognize their own mistakes while hearing about others'.

And read the letter from Laodicea so you guys can read it too. Some people say it wasn't a letter from Paul to them but rather from them to Paul. Because he didn't say "to the Laodiceans", but "from Laodicea", meaning it was written there.

And tell Archippus: 'Make sure you complete the task you received in the Lord'. Why doesn't he write directly to him? Maybe a simple reminder is all he needed, to be more eager in his duties.

"This greeting is in my own hand—Paul." This is a sign of authenticity and friendship, to see the actual handwriting and to feel connected.

"Remember my chains." Wow, what an encouragement! Just this can motivate them for any challenge and make them braver in their struggles. Not only braver but also feel more connected to him. "Grace be with you. Amen."

Id with much modesty and grace, and eyelids crowned with blue, both above and below, the girl herself as if animated, her forehead shining, her cheeks again beneath. Reaching a precise shade of red, lying smooth like polished marble, and perfectly even; then it showed me Paul in tears. I was drawn away from the former sight to this one, for from these eyes shone a spiritual beauty. For that, indeed, causes young souls to stand in awe, it ignites and burns; but this calms them down. Seeing his eyes, one cultivates a more beautiful soul, pulls at the heart, fills it with philosophy and much compassion, and can soften even a diamond-hard spirit. With these tears, the Church is nourished, souls are planted; even if there's fire, these tears can extinguish it, both tangible and physical. These tears can quench the fiery darts of the Wicked One.

So let's remember his tears and laugh at all our present troubles. Christ himself blessed tears when he said: "Blessed are those who mourn, and blessed are those who weep, for they shall laugh" (Luke 6:21). Prophets like Isaiah and Jeremiah shed tears too; one said: "Let me be, I will weep bitterly" (Isaiah 22:4), and the other: "Oh, that my head were water, and my eyes a fountain of tears" (Jeremiah 9:1), as if natural tears weren't enough. Nothing is sweeter than these tears; they are more delightful than any laughter.

Those who mourn know how much comfort there is in it. Let's not think of it as something to avoid, but rather something to be sought after. Not to make others fall into sin, but to be moved by the sins of others, let's remember these tears, these bonds. Indeed, even upon his bonds, tears fell; but he did not allow himself to feel pleasure from being freed from his chains because of the death that destroys those who are bound.

For he also felt pain for them; for he was a disciple of the one who wept. "A priest of the Jews did not worry that he would be crucified, but rather that they were losing themselves. And it's not just him acting this way, but he also encourages others, saying: 'Do not weep for me, daughters of Jerusalem'" (Luke 23:28). These eyes have seen paradise, these eyes have seen the third heaven; but I do not call them blessed for this sight as much as for those tears through which I saw Christ. That truly is a blessing.

For even he himself is honoured because of it, saying: "Have I not seen our Lord Jesus Christ?" But to cry in this way is even more blessed. Many have shared in the vision, and Christ again calls those who have not seen but believed blessed; but not many have achieved this. For if staying here for Christ's sake is more necessary than going to him for the salvation of others, then to see him and to lament for them is more necessary.

If to be with him, even to be in hell for him, is more desirable, and to be apart from him for his sake is more to be longed for (for this is what he said: "I could wish that I myself were accursed from Christ" [Romans 9:3]), much more then is it to weep for him. "I have not ceased to admonish everyone with tears," he says (Acts 20:31). Why? Not because he feared dangers; but as someone sitting beside a sick person, not knowing the outcome, would weep out of longing, fearing lest they slip away from life; so he, when he saw weakness and could not scold, would finally weep.

This is what Christ did, so that even the tears might be honoured; if someone sinned, he reprimanded them; if the rebuked one spat at him and leapt away, he wept, so that he might draw them back even in this way. Let us remember these tears; in this way let us raise our daughters, in this way our sons, weeping when we see them in distress.

Those who wish to be in love, remember Paul's tears and sigh; those who feel blessed, those who are in their chambers, those in pleasure, remember these things; those who are in . Mourn, but change your tears of grief to tears of another kind. It's not the dead that we should grieve for.

But those who are lost to us while still alive. Should I speak of other kinds of tears? Timothy also wept; he was a student of his and so writing to him, he said: "Remembering your tears, that I may be filled with joy." Many also weep from pleasure. Such is the nature of pleasure, especially when it's intense; thus, tears from such pain aren't burdensome, but far better than those shed for worldly pleasures.

Listen to the Prophet saying: "The Lord has heard the voice of my weeping" (Psalm 6:8). Where are tears not useful? In prayers, in advice? But we throw them away, not using them for their intended purpose. When we comfort a brother who is sinning, we must weep, cut to the heart and groaning; when we advise someone who doesn't pay attention, but is being destroyed, we must weep. These are the tears of philosophy; but when someone becomes poor, when they are physically ill, or when they die, no more tears—these are not worth our tears.

Just as we criticise laughter used at the wrong time; so too with tears, misusing them inappropriately. For the virtue of each thing is shown when it is brought to its appropriate work; but when it is brought to what is alien to it, it no longer shines. For instance, wine is given for merriment, not for drunkenness; bread for nourishment, tears for procreation. Just as these things are misused when consumed improperly, so are tears. Let it be a rule that these [tears] are to be used only in prayers and admonitions; and see how desirable the thing will become. Nothing washes away sins like tears. They also make this physical appearance beautiful; for they draw the onlooker to compassion and make it dignified for us.

There is nothing more pleasing than eyes that have cried. For this is the noblest and most beautiful part of us and it is of the soul. So then, seeing it as if we see the soul mourning, we are moved. These things have not been said to you simply, but so that you would not participate in marriages, dances, and choirs of satanic nature.

See what the devil has found: Since the nature of the stage and the indecencies there took women away, he introduced into the women's quarters the things of the theatre, I speak of soft and immoral men. This pollution the law of marriage has introduced; rather, not the law of marriage, God forbid, but our own folly. What are you doing, friend? Don't you realise what you are involved in? You should lead a woman towards modesty and child-rearing; so what then do prostitutes have to do with this?

They aim to amplify the joy, it is said, to make the happiness greater. But isn't this foolishness? You insult the bride, you insult the invited guests. If they find delight in such behaviour, it's an insult in itself. If seeing women behaving indecently incites some kind of ambition, why don't you drag the bride herself to see as well? It is altogether improper and shameful to bring effeminate men and dancers into your home, introducing all the pomp of Satanic influence. "Remember my chains," he says (Philemon 1:13).

Marriage is a bond defined by God; a prostitute represents its breaking and dissolution. Others may brighten up a wedding with lavish banquets and garments—I do not cut back on these so as not to seem too severe; and indeed, a water jug was sufficient for Rebekah, but I do not cut back. One may brighten up with clothes, one may bring in the presence of honourable men and women. What need is there for those jesters, those monstrosities? Say what you hear from them. But do you blush to speak it? You blush, and yet you force others to do it?

If it's good, why don't you do it yourself? And if it's shameful, why do you force another to do it? Everything must be filled with modesty, dignity, and decorum;

but now I see the opposite: they leap as camels and donkeys. A chamber is suitable only for a virgin. But it's meagre, he says. Because it's meagre, it should also be proper; let her demeanour be her wealth if she has no dowry to bring.

Why do you make her even more contemptible by your conduct? I praise the fact that virgins come to honour their peers, that women come to honour the one chosen among them; this is well established.

For these are two groups: the virgins and the married; the latter give away, the former receive. The bride stands between them, neither a virgin nor yet a wife; for she is leaving the one group to join the other. "Why the prostitutes, you ask? They should be hidden away during a wedding, they should be buried out of sight, for prostitution is the corruption of marriage, and yet we bring them into marriages.

Whenever you do something, you even predict the opposite outcome; for example, when you sow seeds or draw wine from the storage pits that should be tart, you wouldn't even respond. But when moderation is present, why do you introduce something sour? For this is what the prostitute is. When you are preparing perfume, you don't allow any foul smell to come near. Marriage is like perfume; why then do you let the stench of filth mix with the making of perfume?

What are you saying? The maiden dances, and isn't she ashamed before her peer? She must be more dignified than her; after all, she came from a cradle, not from a wrestling ring. The maiden should not even appear at weddings at all. Don't you see in royal courts that the honoured are inside with the king, while the dishonoured are outside? And you should be inside with the bride.

But remain pure at home; don't parade your virginity. Each side is present, one showing the gifts they provide, the other ensuring they are protected; why do you disgrace virginity? For if you are such, the groom will suspect the same about her; if you want to love, these things are for the grocer, the vegetable seller, and the craftsman. Isn't this a disgrace?

It is shameful to behave indecently, even if you are a king's daughter. Isn't poverty an excuse? Isn't your profession an excuse? Even if a girl is a slave, let her remain in purity; for in Christ Jesus there is neither slave nor free (Galatians 3:28). Isn't marriage a theatre? It is a mystery and a symbol of something greater; even if you do not respect it, respect what it symbolises.

"Okay, so there's this huge mystery we're talking about," he says. "And I'm connecting it directly to Christ and the Church. Think of the Church as a symbol, right? And you want to bring what... scandals into it? No way. If we say that neither single nor married people are dancing, who's left to dance? Nobody. Why would there even be a need to dance?

In the old Greek mysteries, dancing was a thing, but in our Christian vibe, it's all about being quiet, proper, and respectful. We're talking about a big deal mystery here; no place for any kind of shady behaviour. What's this mystery about? When people come together in this context, they're not just hanging out—they're becoming one. That's what marriage is.

Why is it that when you walk into a holy place, there's no dancing, no loud music, just a lot of quiet and peace? But when you join together in marriage, instead of representing something lifeless or just another person on Earth, you're actually creating an image of God Himself. So why introduce chaos into this holy scene, disturbing the peace and being disrespectful?

Here's the thing: when two people come together in marriage, they're set to become one body. It's all about the mystery of love. If the two don't become one, they can't really fulfil their purpose. It's only when they unite that they truly become productive. What do we learn from this? There's a ton of strength in unity. God, in His wisdom, split the one into two right from the start. And to show that even after being divided, they're still one, He didn't make it so one could do it all alone when it comes to creating new life. One isn't really one yet; it's only half. And clearly, half can't create like it could before. You see the mystery of marriage?

God made one from one, and then He took these two and made them one again, continuing to create one human at a time. Because now, from one, a person is born. A woman and a man come together in a unity that reflects how things are meant to be.

The Sacred Mystery of Marriage

"People aren't just two separate beings, but rather one single being; and you can see this truth from different angles. Just think about it like with Jacob, with Mary the mother of Christ, or when it's said: 'Male and female He created them.'" (Genesis 1:27) If one is the head and the other the body, how can they be two? That's why one takes the role of a student and the other a teacher; one leads, and the other follows.

You can also see from the very way our bodies are put together that we are meant to be one. We were made from the same stuff, like two halves of the same whole. That's why a helper is called for, to show that together, they are one; that's why the bond between a husband and wife is held in such high regard, even more so than the bond with parents—to show that they are one.

Just as a parent rejoices at their daughter or son getting married, seeing it as a union with a part of their own body, even though it costs a fortune and might reduce their wealth, they still don't like the idea of them staying single. Just like when flesh is cut from flesh, each part is incomplete for creating life, so is each one incomplete for making a full life on their own. That's why the prophet says: 'They are a remnant of your spirit.' (Malachi 2:15) But how do they become one flesh?

Just as if you take the purest gold and mix it with another gold, they become one. Similarly, in marriage, the woman embraces the sweetest joy, nurtures it, warms it, and returns what she has taken in, together with the man. And the child is like a bridge between them. So, the three become one flesh, with the child joining each to the other.

It's like if there were two cities separated by a river, and they become one city when a bridge connects them from both sides. It's the same here, and even more so because the bridge is made from each side. And in this way, they are one, just as the body and the head are one body; for though the neck separates them, it doesn't really separate them as much as it joins them, being in the middle and bringing them together.

"It's the same as if a dance group was split, and one part of the group joined from one side and another from the right. Imagine if someone decided to become one; like those close-knit friends who, when they stretch out their hands to each other, they're no longer two but become one. Because when hands are extended, they're not separate anymore.

That's exactly why it was said so clearly: it's not 'they will be one flesh,' but 'they will unite into one flesh,' clearly referring to the unity of a child. So what then, when there isn't a child, aren't they still two? It's obvious: the blending of two people does this, pouring and mixing together both bodies. Just like when you pour fragrance into oil, you make it all one, the same happens here.

I know that many feel ashamed of these things being discussed; and the reason for this shame is indecency and lack of restraint. The misconception that marriages are corrupted has tainted the institution; because marriage is honourable, and the marital bed is pure. "Marriage is honourable in all, and the bed undefiled," (Hebrews 13:4) Why feel shame for something honourable? Why blush at what is pure? These are the claims of heretics, of those who have brought corruption. That's why I want to cleanse this view, to restore the honour it deserves, to silence the mouths of heretics. They insult God's gift, the root of our existence. For there is a lot of muck and mud around the root.

So let's clear it away with reason. Hang in there, because just like someone who handles mud puts up with the stink, we need to deal with this. I want to show you that we shouldn't be embarrassed by these things, but by what you're doing; you leave aside those things you should be ashamed of and feel embarrassed about these others; aren't you then criticising God who arranged things this way?

Let me explain how this is also a mystery of the Church: Christ came to the Church, was born from it, and entered into a spiritual union with it. "I promised you to one husband, to Christ, as a pure virgin," (2 Corinthians 11:2) says the scripture. And that we are from Him, listen to this: "We are members of His body, of His flesh and of His bones." (Ephesians 5:30) With all this in mind, let's not be embarrassed by this great mystery.

Marriage is a symbol of Christ's presence, but you're getting drunk? Tell me, if you saw an image of the king, would you be ashamed of it? Of course not. Things concerning marriage might seem trivial, but they are often the cause of great evils.

Everything fills with wrongdoing. "Let there be no filthiness nor foolish talk nor crude joking, which are out of place," (Ephesians 5:4) says the scripture. All those things, vulgarity, foolish talk, and jesting, are not just inappropriate, but they're excessive. Because the matter at hand is a craft, and great praise is due to those who practise it skillfully; sin has become a craft. We don't just commit sins, but we do it with eagerness, with knowledge; and the devil strategizes his tactics accordingly.

Where there is drunkenness, there is disorder; where there is filthy talk, the devil is present bringing his own contributions. By engaging in these things, tell me, do you serve the mystery of Christ, or are you calling on the devil? You might think I'm a nuisance. But this is also because of the great distortion, that even the one who reprimands is received with laughter as being too stern.

Don't you hear Paul saying, "Whether you eat or drink, or whatever you do, do all to the glory of God?" (1 Corinthians 10:31) But you are doing things for dishonour and disgrace. Don't you hear the Prophet saying, "Serve the Lord with fear, and rejoice with trembling?" (Psalm 2:11) But you're being careless.

Can't we have joy and still be safe? Want to hear about good members? Ideally, you wouldn't even need to, but I'll come down to your level if you want; don't listen to the satanic, but to the spiritual. Want to see dancing? Look at the dance of the angels. And how can you see this, you ask? If you drive these things out, Christ will also come to this marriage; and where Christ is present, there too is the dance of the angels. If you wish, even now He can perform miracles, just as He did then; He can now turn.

Pay attention to the kind of marriage you seek. First off, for your daughter, look for a man who's truly a man, a real supporter, someone who'll be the head to her body, not a master treating her like a servant, but as if he's receiving a daughter of his own.

Don't hunt for money, flashy family status, or the size of his hometown. All that stuff is extra. What you want is someone with a respect for the soul, kindness, true understanding, and fear of God, if you want your daughter to live with joy. If you go after wealth, you won't just fail to benefit her, you'll actually harm her, turning a free woman into a servant. She won't enjoy the gold as much as she'll despise being in servitude.

So don't look for these things. Try to find someone of equal standing; if that's not possible, it's better to settle for someone less wealthy than more, if you want to give your daughter to a partner, not a boss. When you've carefully checked out a guy's character and are about to marry off your daughter, ask Christ to be present. He won't be ashamed; it's a mystery worthy of His attendance. Especially then, ask for such a suitor.

Don't be worse than Abraham's servant, who went on a long journey and knew where to turn for help and therefore succeeded in everything. When you're searching for the right man, pray. Tell God: "You manage it. I trust You with this task," and He, honoured by your trust, will repay you. Do two things: entrust it to Him, and look for the kind of man He would want for her—decent, self-controlled.

When organising the wedding, don't fuss over houses, mirrors, and fancy clothes. It's not a show, you're not parading your daughter around. Instead, brighten the home with those inside, invite neighbours, friends, and relatives. Call on those you know to be kind, and encourage them to be sufficient for the gathering. No need for flashy performers; that's just extra expense and frankly, looks bad. Invite Christ before everyone else.

You know why you're inviting Him? Because, He says, "Whatever you do for the least of these, you do for Me." (Matthew 25:40) Don't think it's unpleasant to invite the poor for Christ's sake; it's unpleasant to invite corrupt people. Calling on the poor can lead to riches, while the other leads to ruin.

Adorn the bride not with gold or glittery things, but with gentleness, modesty, and the usual clothes. Red cheeks from modesty are worth more than all the gold and elaborate decorations, and not chasing after those things. Let there be no chaos, no uproar; let the groom be called, and let him receive the bride. The best. The bride is radiant; everything that follows is all about her.

You see, watching everything fall apart is a cause for despair, seeing the home deserted is a reason for gloom. There's Christ on one side, and Satan on the other; over there is celebration, but here is worry; there is pleasure, but here is sorrow; there is spending, but here is nothing of the sort; there is indecency, but here is decency; there is envy, but here is plenty; there is drunkenness, but here is sobriety. Here lies salvation, here lies self-control.

Keeping all these things in mind, let's put a stop to evil just to this point, so that we may please God, and may we be deemed worthy to receive the good things promised to those who love Him, through the grace and kindness of our Lord Jesus Christ. With Him, to the Father and the Holy Spirit, be glory, power, and honour, now and forever, and for all eternity. Amen.

Chapter 2

MUTUAL DUTIES AND RESPECT IN MARRIAGE

St John Chrysostom
Homily 19 (1 Corinthians 7)

"Now about what you wrote to me: it's good for a man not to touch a woman. But to avoid immorality, each man should have his own wife, and each woman her own husband."

(1 Corinthians 7:1-2)

After addressing the three most difficult issues, one being the division in the church, the second the immoral person, and the third the greedy person, the author turns to more peaceful discourse. They place between them advice and counsel about marriage and virginity, giving the listener a break from more burdensome topics.

In contrast, in the second letter, the author starts with more peaceful topics and ends with more serious ones. Here, after completing the discussion about virginity, they again turn to more challenging subjects, not always arranging them in order, but varying the discourse as needed by the time and circumstances. This is why it says, 'Now about what you wrote to me.' They had written to him, asking if it's necessary to abstain from women, or not.

In response, while also laying down the law about marriage, he introduces the discussion about virginity: 'It's good for a man not to touch a woman.' If you seek what's excellent and superior, he says, it's better not to have any dealings with women at all. But if you seek safety and help with your weakness, then engage in marriage. Since it's likely, as it happens now, that a man might want this and a woman no longer, or vice versa, notice how he discusses both.

Some say this advice was specifically for priests. However, based on the following, I wouldn't say this is the case. He didn't make the advice universally applicable. If he was writing only to priests, he would've said, 'It's good for a teacher not to touch a woman.' But instead, he makes it universal, saying 'It's good for a man,' not just for a priest. And again, 'Are you free from a wife? Do not seek a wife.' He doesn't say, 'You, the priest and teacher,' but leaves it undefined; the entire discussion proceeds in this manner.

"Because of immoralities, each man should have his own wife, and this leads to self-control and mutual consent. The husband should give the respect that is owed to his wife, and the wife should do the same to her husband. What is this respect?

A woman doesn't have control over her own body, but she is both a servant and mistress of her husband. If she withdraws from proper servitude, she offends God. If she wants to withdraw, she should only do it with her husband's permission, and even then only for a short time. The writer calls this an obligation to show that no one is his own master, but rather they are servants of each other.

So, if you are tempted by immorality, say, 'My body is not my own, but my wife's.' The wife should say the same to those who would tempt her: 'My body is not mine, but my husband's.' If a man or woman doesn't control their body, they should control their money even more. Listen, all of you who have husbands or wives. If it is not proper to have control over one's own body, it is even less proper to have control over money.

In other places, the man is given leadership, both in the New Testament and the Old Testament, saying, 'Your desire will be for your husband, and he will rule over you.' (Genesis 3:16) But Paul, dividing and writing, says, 'Husbands, love your wives, and the wife should respect her husband.' (Ephesians 5:33) Here, there is no more or less, but one authority.

Don't deprive each other of what's fair. Someone once wisely said, "Don't withhold what is owed," to stress the importance of obeying rules. If something is taken unwillingly, it's wrong, but if taken willingly, it's not. Even if you persuade me to give you something of mine, I don't consider it wrong. Taking something by force is wrong, something some people, especially women, do, committing a big mistake.

Love, peace, and harmony should be valued above all, because they are more powerful. Let's look at the situation of a man and a woman. If the woman has control and goes against the man's wishes, what happens if he rebels or becomes angry? What's the benefit of self-control if love is broken? Nothing. It only leads to insults, issues, and conflict. In a home where the husband and wife are at odds, nothing is worse. It's like a ship tossed in a storm with the captain and sailor fighting.

The advice here is not to deprive each other, except by agreement for a time for fasting and prayer. But if this interferes with your prayers together, how can you find the time? You can talk to your spouse and pay attention to prayer, but this must be done with precise self-control. It's not just about praying, but about setting aside time for it, without impurity. Get together again, so Satan doesn't tempt you. The devil isn't the only one working on adultery; there's also your lack of self-control.

The speaker says this as a suggestion, not a command, wishing all to be as self-controlled as he is. Everyone has their own gift from God, in different ways. Since he blamed them strongly, he comforts them again, saying that each one has their unique gift from God. You shouldn't be misled.

I have some advice for married people, and this isn't coming from me, but from the Lord Himself.

Now, let's talk about a clear rule set down by Christ. It's about not leaving one's wife except in cases of infidelity. It's not just what I think, but what Christ explicitly stated. So when I say "I" or "not I," I'm pointing out a difference in authority. Don't think that these are merely human words, for I also think that I have the Spirit of God.

So what did the Lord command married people? A wife shouldn't leave her husband. If she does separate, she should remain unmarried or be reconciled with her husband, and a man should not leave his wife. Since divisions can happen for many reasons, like lack of self-control or small-mindedness, it's best not to start in the first place, but if it does happen, the wife should stay with her husband. It's not necessarily about intimacy but not introducing another man into the relationship.

To the rest, I say, not the Lord: If any brother has an unbelieving wife, and she is willing to live with him, he should not divorce her. And a woman who has an unbelieving husband, if he's willing to live with her, should not leave him. Just as in discussing separation from immoral people, he made the matter easier, saying, "Not at all meaning the immoral people of this world;" so here, he considered much ease, saying, "If anyone has an unbelieving husband or wife, do not leave them."

What are you saying? If he's an unbeliever, he may stay with his wife; if he's immoral, no longer? Yet unfaithfulness is worse than immorality. Immorality may be less, but God cares deeply for what is yours. He demonstrates this even during sacrifices, saying, 'Leave your offering, and make peace with your brother.' This applies to the one who owes ten thousand talents as well. Although one man owed him ten thousand talents and was not punished, he punished another who demanded a hundred dinars from a fellow servant.

Then, so that the woman does not fear becoming impure through the union, he says, 'For the unbelieving husband is sanctified by the wife, and the unbelieving wife is sanctified by the husband.' Even though one who unites with a prostitute becomes one body, it is clear that one who unites with an idolater is also one body. Indeed, they are one body, but it does not become impure; instead, the purity of the woman overcomes the impurity of the man, and the purity of the believing husband also overcomes the impurity of the unbelieving wife.

So, how is it that impurity is overcome here, and the union is allowed, but the man does not cast out his wife if she is unfaithful? It's because here there is hope to save what is lost through marriage, while there the marriage has already been dissolved; and there both are ruined, while here only one is guilty. Let me explain what I mean: The woman who has been unfaithful even once is defiled. If, then, the one who unites with a prostitute becomes one body, and he also becomes defiled by joining with an unfaithful woman, then all purity is avoided. But it's not like that here. How so? The idolater is impure, but the woman is not impure. If she were involved with him in this way, as he is impure, I mean in his ungodliness, she too would become impure. But now the idolater is impure in one way, and in another..."

"In the matter of marriage, the wife shares in partnership, where nothing is unclean. For marriage is the union of bodies, just like a community. Again, there is hope that the man might be welcomed back by the woman, for she is familiar to him; but it is not very easy for the other man. How can the one who dishonoured him in the past, who became another's, and who made the rightful aspects of marriage disappear, be able to call back the wronged one, treating him as a stranger?

Again, after unfaithfulness, the man is not considered a man; but here, even if the wife worships idols, the man's right is not destroyed. She does not simply live with the unbelieving man, but with the willing one; that is why it was said, 'He also consents to live with her.' Tell me, what harm is there, when the virtues of piety remain untouched, and there are good hopes concerning the unbeliever, to keep those who have already been united, without introducing unnecessary conflicts?"

The original text likely holds a nuanced philosophical or theological discussion. "Should someone introduce this question? It doesn't discuss those who haven't yet come together, but those who have already done so. It doesn't say, 'If anyone wants to take an unbeliever,' but 'If anyone has an unbeliever.' For example, if someone after getting married accepts the word of godliness, and then one part remains in disbelief but still loves to live together, let them not be separated. For the unbeliever is sanctified by the wife. Such is the abundance of your purity.

So then, is the Greek person holy? Not at all! It doesn't say, 'He is holy,' but 'He is sanctified by the wife.' This is said, not to show him as holy, but to remove the wife's fear out of abundance, and lead him to desire the truth. For it's not the bodies that are impure, which are shared, but the choice and thoughts. Then there's proof: if you, remaining impure, give birth, the child is not just from you, so is it impure or half-pure? Now it's not impure. So it adds, 'Since your children are impure; now they are holy,' that is, not impure. He called it holy, again expelling such suspicion with the richness of words. But if the unbeliever separates, let them separate.

For here adultery is not the issue. What does it mean, 'If the unbeliever separates'? Like if he orders you to sacrifice and share in his impiety because of marriage, or to retreat, it's better to break the marriage, and not godliness. So it adds, 'The brother or sister is not bound in such cases.' If every day he fights and causes wars for this, it says, better to be released. For God has called us to peace. He alone gave the reason, just like the one committing adultery. 'For what do you know, woman, if you'll save your husband?' Again towards, 'Do not let him go,' it says this. 'For if he doesn't rebel, stay,' it says, 'for there's also a gain; stay, and advise and persuade; for no teacher will be as strong as a wife.' And neither does he impose a necessity on her and absolutely demand this from her, so as not to burden her again, nor does he order to despair, but leaves it up in the air with the uncertainty of the future, saying, 'For what do you know, woman, if you'll save your husband?' and 'What do you know, man, if you'll save your wife?' and again, 'If not to each as God has distributed, each as the Lord has called, so let him walk. Were you called being circumcised? Do not become uncircumcised.'

Were you called to follow the faith when you were not circumcised? Don't worry about getting circumcised. Circumcision or not being circumcised doesn't matter; what matters is obeying God's commands. Stay as you were when you were called. Were you a slave when you were called? Don't let that bother you. But if you can gain your freedom, go ahead and use it. These things don't matter to faith; so don't argue or make a fuss about them, for faith has done away with these things. Each person should remain as they were when they were called. Were you called to faith while married to someone who doesn't believe? Stay with them; don't throw them out because of faith. Were you a slave when you were called? Don't worry; continue to serve. Were you not circumcised when you were called? Stay that way. Were you circumcised when you came to believe? Stay that way. This is how God has assigned to each person, for these things are not hindrances to devout living. You may be a slave, another may have a spouse who doesn't believe, and another may be circumcised. Wow! Where does this place slavery! Just as circumcision doesn't help, nor does not being circumcised hurt, neither does slavery nor freedom.

To make this even clearer, the writer says, "But if you can become free, rather serve." This means, better be a servant. Why does he advise someone who could be free to remain a slave? To show that slavery does not harm but even helps. I know that some say that "rather serve" means to be free, saying, "If you can gain your freedom, gain it." But this is very contrary to the way the author meant it. He wouldn't encourage a slave, showing him that he hasn't been wronged, to become free. For someone might say, "What then? If I can't, have I been wronged and made lesser?" Therefore, this is not what the author is saying.

"But as I said, wanting to show that nothing more comes to one who has become free, he says: 'Even if you are the master of being set free, remain a slave even more.' Then he adds the reason: 'For the one called a slave in the Lord is the Lord's freedman; similarly, the one called free is a slave of Christ. For in Christ, both are equal; for you are a slave of Christ, just as your master is. So how is the slave free? Because He freed you not only from sin but also from outside slavery, remaining a slave. For He does not allow the slave to be a slave, nor a person to remain in slavery; this is what's amazing. And how is the slave free, remaining a slave? When he is rid of suffering and the diseases of the soul, when he despises money and anger and other such passions. You were bought with a price; do not become slaves of men. This word is not spoken only to servants but also to free people. For there is being a slave without being a slave, and being free while being a slave. And how, being a slave, is he not a slave? When he does everything for God, when he does not pretend or do things just to please people; that is, being free while serving people. Or how, again, being free, does one become a slave? When he serves men some wicked service or for gluttony, or for desire for money, or for power. For such a one is more slavish, even if he is free.

Consider both of these things: Joseph was a slave, but not a slave to men; therefore even in slavery, he was all He was even freer among the free. He didn't obey his mistress, and did whatever he wanted. Yet, she was free too, but more enslaved than anyone else, flattering and pleading with her servant; but she couldn't persuade him to do what he didn't want to do. So the issue wasn't about slavery but the highest form of freedom. What held him back from virtue because of slavery? Let both slaves and free listen: Who was enslaved? The one being asked, or the one asking? The one pleading, or the one disregarding the plea? God has set boundaries for slaves; how far they must keep them has been determined, and they must not overstep them. When the master commands nothing against God, they must follow and obey; but no further. Thus, a slave becomes free. But if you go further, even if you're free, you become a slave. He warns about this, saying: Do not become slaves to men.

But if not this, if he ordered to abandon masters and become quarrelsome and free, how did he advise saying: Each should remain in the condition in which he was called? And elsewhere, "Let those who are slaves under the yoke regard their own masters as worthy of all honour, so that the name of God and our doctrine will not be spoken against. Those who have believers as their masters must not be disrespectful to them because they are brothers; but must serve them all the more, because those who partake of the benefit are believers and beloved." (1 Timothy 6:1-2) Ephesians and Colossians also command the same laws. Therefore, it's clear that this doesn't abolish slavery but that from wickedness, even to free people, which is the hardest slavery if someone is enslaved to it.

Why were Joseph's brothers more enslaved than any slave, although they were free? Didn't they lie to their father, deceive traders, and their brother? But the free man is not like this; he is truthful everywhere and in everything. Nothing could enslave him: not bonds, not slavery, not the love of a mistress, not being in a foreign land. But he remained free everywhere. For this is the most important freedom, that it even shines through slavery. This is Christianity: it grants freedom within slavery. Just as an invulnerable body shows itself as invulnerable when it takes a blow without serious injury, so does a truly free person when, even having masters, they are not enslaved.

Therefore, it commands to remain a slave. If it's impossible to be a slave and a proper Christian, the Greeks accuse our religion of a great weakness; as if they learn that true faith is not harmed by slavery; people will marvel at this message. For if death doesn't harm us, nor whips, nor chains, much less will slavery, fire, iron, countless tyrannies, diseases, poverty, and wild beasts, and many things more dreadful than these, have not harmed the faithful but have made them even stronger. And how can slavery harm us, one might ask? It's not this kind of slavery that harms us, dear one, but the slavery of sin. If you are not a slave to this kind of slavery, you'll be bold and joyful; nobody will be able to wrong you, having a free spirit. But if you are a slave to it, even if you are a thousand times free, the freedom will be of no benefit to you.

What benefit is it, tell me, when you are not a slave to a man, but to the people "Why do you bow and submit yourself? People often know how to show mercy, but those masters never tire of your destruction. Do you serve a man? But he also serves you, taking care of your food, watching over your health, clothing, shoes, and all other needs. You are not so afraid of offending your master as he is of neglecting something necessary for you. He lies down, but you stand. What of it? This is not only his concern but yours as well. Often, while you are comfortably asleep, he not only stands but endures many struggles in the marketplace and stays awake more fretfully than you. Consider what Joseph endured from his mistress, driven by her desires. He did not do what she wanted; she did everything her lust demanded, not stopping until she had disgraced herself. What master, what savage tyrant, orders such things? 'Beg your slave,' it says, 'entreat your captive, flatter the one bought with silver; if he spits at you, endure it again; if you tell him many times and he does not bear it, watch for his absence, force yourself, and become a laughingstock.' What is more disgraceful or shameful than these words? If you achieve nothing even so, then deceive and cheat your housemate.

See how base, how ugly these commands are, how harsh and brutal and mad. What does the master command like lust commanded that queen back then? But she dared not disobey. Joseph endured nothing like this but quite the opposite, things that brought glory and honour.

Do you want to see another man ordered around by a harsh mistress, not daring to disobey? Consider Cain, all that he was ordered to do by envy. She ordered him to kill his brother, lie to God, grieve his father, be shameless, and he did everything, he did not disobey at all.

What lessons would people learn, that slavery does not harm piety? They would admire the proclamation. If death, whips, bonds, fire, and iron do not harm us, if countless tyrants, diseases, poverty, and beasts, things harder than these, did not harm the faithful but made them even stronger, how can slavery harm us? It is not this slavery that harms, beloved, but the natural slavery of sin.

"Why do you bow down to yourself? People often know how to spare each other, but those masters never tire of your destruction. Are you a servant to a man? But your master also serves you, managing your food, taking care of your health, your clothing, and your footwear, and worrying about everything else. You are not so afraid of offending the master, as he is afraid of neglecting something necessary for you. But he lies down, and you have stood firm. And what of this? For this isn't only with him but also with you. Many times indeed, while you were lying down and sleeping comfortably, he didn't just stand still but endured countless hardships in the marketplace, and watched more painfully than you.

What, then? Joseph suffered something like this at the hands of his mistress, just like from that desire? For he did not do what she wanted him to do; but she did everything that her mistress, I mean lust, commanded, and didn't stop until she had shamed her. What kind of master orders these things? What cruel tyrant? 'Plead with your slave,' he says, 'beg the captive, flatter the man bought with money; and if he spits at you, keep going, even if you ask many times and he doesn't listen, watch for an opportunity, and force yourself on him, and become a laughingstock.' What could be more dishonourable, more shameful than these words? But if you don't achieve anything even this way, then deceive and cheat your housemate.

See how ungentlemanly, how shameful these orders are, how cruel and mad. What kind of thing does the master order, what did lust command the queen then? But she didn't dare to disobey. Joseph endured nothing like this but all the opposite, which brought glory and honour. Do you want to see another man who was ordered much by a difficult mistress, and didn't dare to disobey? Think of Cain, what he was commanded by envy. She commanded him to kill his brother, to lie to God, to grieve his father, to be shameless, and he did everything, and didn't disobey anything.

And why are you surprised if this mistress has so much power over one person? Often she has destroyed whole communities. The women of the Midianites almost took the Jews captive, captivated by their beauty. Therefore Paul, expelling this slavery, said: "Do not become slaves of men." (1 Corinthians 7:23) That is, "Don't obey men who order absurd things, but not even yourselves."

Then he lifts his thoughts and makes them lofty, saying, "About virgins, I have no command from the Lord; but

I give my judgement as one who has obtained mercy from the Lord to be trustworthy." (1 Corinthians 7:25) Proceeding by way and order he also later mentions virginity. For having trained them in self-control with words and set them in order, he goes on to something greater, saying, "I have no command, but I think it is good." Why? For the same reason that he has set for self-control. "Are you bound to a wife? Do not seek release."

"Then, so that this doesn't seem like a law, he added: 'But if you do marry, you have not sinned.'" (1 Corinthians 7:28) Then he explains the present situation, the existing necessity, the limited time, and the difficulties.

For marriage brings many things, which he touched upon here and in his speech about self-control, saying there that "The wife does not have authority over herself," (1 Corinthians 7:4) and here saying, "You are bound. But if you do marry, you have not sinned." It's not about choosing virginity; for she has already sinned. For if widows face judgement for entering into second marriages, how much more so do virgins, if they once choose widowhood? But those who do this will have physical hardship. But pleasure too, he says. But look how he limited even this pleasure by the shortness of time, saying, "The time has been shortened." (1 Corinthians 7:29) That is, "We are being called away and to depart soon, and yet you are running more inwardly." And even if marriage had nothing burdensome, still, it would be necessary to hurry to what's coming. But when it also has hardship, why add a burden? Why take on so much weight, when even after taking it, you need to live as though not having it? For he says, "Those who have wives should live as though they do not." (1 Corinthians 7:29) Then after saying something about the future, he brought the conversation back to the present. For indeed. The matters at hand are spiritual.

Some are concerned with human affairs, while others focus on the matters of God, or on the present life. I want you to be without worry. Still, even so, you must make your own decisions. For the one who insists on proving a point seems not to trust his own words. Therefore, it seems that he went on more by permission than by force, saying, "What I'm telling you is for your own good, not to trap you, but to guide you towards proper behaviour and good conduct."

Let the young women listen, because being a virtuous young woman is not just a matter of status. For the one who worries about worldly things might not even be considered virtuous or well-behaved. Because, as it has been said, both women and young unmarried women have differences, and this defines how they are different from one another. It doesn't talk about marriage or self-control but about being concerned with many things or very few. Mixing with others isn't bad, but being hindered from philosophy is.

If someone thinks that it's improper to speak about young women, here it seems to speak in favour of marriage, but mostly about being a virtuous young woman. It even allows for marriage a second time, saying only, "In the Lord." What does this mean? With modesty, with decorum. We need these everywhere, and we must pursue them; otherwise, we cannot see God. "Pursue peace and holiness, without which no one will see the Lord." (Hebrews 12:14)

If we pass over the discussions about being virtuous, let none of us hesitate to criticise. For we have a complete book about this subject, and having gone through it with the attention it deserves, we thought it would be redundant to repeat it here. Therefore, directing the listener over those parts, here we will say that we must pursue self-control. "For pursue peace," it says, "and holiness, without which no one will see the Lord." (Hebrews 12:14)

Therefore, let us strive to see Him, whether we are virtuous young women, whether in the first marriage or in the second, let us pursue this, so we may obtain the kingdom of heaven, by the grace and love of our Lord Jesus Christ, with whom, to the Father and the Holy Spirit be glory, power, honour, now and forever, and to the ages of ages. Amen.

Chapter 3

GOD-CENTERED MARRIAGE

St John Chrysostom
Homily 20 (Ephesians 5:22-23)

"Wives, submit to your own husbands, as to the Lord. For the husband is head of the wife, as also Christ is head of the church; and He is the Savior of the body".

Women, respect your husbands like you would respect the Lord, because the husband is the head of the household, just like Christ is the head of the Church. He is also the saviour of the body. Just like the Church respects the Lord, so should wives respect their husbands in all things.

An intelligent man once said in a list of blessings that one blessing is 'A woman acting in harmony with her man.' God has always had a special plan for couples; He even says, 'He made them male and female.' [Genesis 1:27] There is no closer relationship than that between a man and a woman who are united as they should be. This love is truly unique. It has both intensity and everlasting nature, revealing a natural desire that binds two bodies together.

See how tightly knit the relationship is? God didn't let any foreign elements come between a man and a woman. First, a woman came from a man, and then men and women came from both. God designed it all carefully. In the same way that a tree is most sturdy when it has one solid trunk and many branches growing from it, so too did God create all of humanity from one man, Adam. This was to prevent us from becoming divided. Love is the ultimate bond that holds us together. This is why we no longer marry our sisters or daughters, to keep this love focused and strong.

Love and relationships are important not just for families but also for entire communities. Nothing shapes our lives quite like the love between a man and a woman. For the sake of this love, people are willing to go to war and even risk their lives. Why do you think the Apostle Paul made such a big deal about this? He said, 'Wives, submit to your own husbands, as to the Lord.' [Ephesians 5:22] This is because when a couple is in harmony, their kids grow up well, their servants are well-behaved, and even their neighbours enjoy the good vibes. Friends and relatives also benefit. But if it's the opposite, everything becomes upside down and chaotic.

It's like when generals are at peace, everything falls into place, but when they are at odds, everything turns to chaos. That's why Paul says, 'Wives, submit to your own husbands, as to the Lord.' [Ephesians 5:22] But wait! Why then does he also say somewhere else, 'Unless someone leaves behind both wife and husband, they can't follow me'? [Matthew 19:29] "If we're supposed to submit to the Lord, how can anyone say it's okay to rebel because of the Lord? It's crucial to understand that the idea of 'submitting' isn't one-size-fits-all. What it really means is that when you serve the Lord, even if not through a man, you're doing it primarily for the Lord.

So when you listen to your husband, think of it as serving the Lord. If someone who rebels against worldly authorities is also going against God's orders, then a wife who doesn't submit to her husband is doing the same thing. God wanted it this way from the start. Think of it like this: the husband is like the head, and the wife is like the body. Just like Christ is the saviour of the Church, the husband is considered the saviour of this 'body.' So wives, submit to your husbands as you would to God, and husbands, love your wives just like Christ loves the Church.

You hear about this idea of submission, and you might admire Paul for how he's trying to shape our lives. But also listen to what's required of you: Men, love your wives." "Love your wives," it says, "just like Christ loved the Church." [Ephesians 5:25] See that? That's the standard for obedience. But wait, it's also the standard for love. You want your wife to listen to you like the Church listens to Christ? Then you should also take care of her like Christ takes care of the Church. Even if it means giving up your life for her, or going through countless hardships, or enduring any kind of suffering, don't back down. Even if you do all this, you're still not doing as much as Christ did. Because you're doing all this for someone you're already united with, while Christ did it for those who were turning away from him and even hating him.

Just like Christ brought people who were rejecting and hating him back to his side with great care—not with threats or insults or fear or anything like that—you should treat your wife the same way. Even if you see her looking down on you or disrespecting you, you can win her over with your undying care, love, and friendship. There's nothing more powerful than these bonds, especially between a man and a woman. You might keep a servant in line with fear, but not even that really works; they could run away at any moment. But the partner you share your life with, the mother of your kids, the source of all your happiness—you should tie those bonds not with fear and threats, but with love and a good attitude.

"What kind of marriage is it when the wife is afraid of her husband? What joy can the husband get from living with a wife as if she were a slave and not free? If you do something good for her, don't blame her. Even Christ didn't do that. He gave himself up for her, to make her holy and pure. Was she impure, flawed, ugly, and cheap before? No matter what kind of wife you have, she's not as different from you as the Church is from Christ. But Christ still loved her, despite her flaws.

Want to know how flawed the Church was? Listen to what Paul said: 'You were once darkness, now you are light in the Lord.' [Ephesians 5:8] You see how dark she was? But look at how bold she was too: 'Living in malice and envy, hated by others and hating one another.' [Titus 3:3] And how impure: 'Disobedient, deceived, enslaved by all kinds of passions and pleasures.' [Titus 3:3] Even though the Church was all these things, Christ still loved her as if she was wonderful and beautiful. He made her beautiful, washed her clean, and didn't ask for anything in return. He wanted to make her pure and blameless. And he did it with the baptism 'in the name of the Father, the Son, and the Holy Spirit.' [Matthew 28:19]

So, don't expect things from your wife that she doesn't have. Everything that the Church has, she got from the Lord: she became glorious and blameless because of him. Don't turn away from your wife because of her flaws. Listen to what the Scripture says: 'The bee is for birds, and its fruit is the beginning of sweetness.' [Sirach 11:3] It's a creation of God; don't insult it, but rather the one who made it.

What should we say about women? Don't praise them for their beauty; praise and hate both belong to undisciplined souls. Seek the beauty of the soul and emulate the bridegroom of the Church (presumably referring to Christ). Outer beauty is full of arrogance and neglect, causing jealousy and making you suspect things wrongly. But does it bring pleasure? Maybe for the first month or two, or at most for a year. Then, the wonder fades due to routine, but the bad things that come with beauty—pride, neglect, arrogance—remain. With someone not focused on physical beauty, love stays strong because it is love of the soul, not the body.

What's better than the sky, tell me? What's better than the stars? Whatever body you mention, it's not as bright; whatever eyes you mention, they're not as radiant. Even angels marvelled at these, and we still do, but not as intensely as before. Such is the power of routine; it doesn't amaze us in the same way. How much more so with a woman? If sickness occurs, everything falls apart instantly. Look for goodwill, moderation, and kindness in a woman. These are the real marks of beauty.

Don't demand or blame her for things she can't control, like her physical appearance; better yet, don't blame her at all. Haven't you seen how many men have ruined their lives with beautiful women? And how many have lived happily into old age with women not especially beautiful? Let's clean the inner stains, remove the inner wrinkles, and get rid of the faults of the soul. This is the kind of beauty that God seeks.

"Let's build a good life, not for ourselves, but for God. Don't seek wealth or outward nobility; instead, focus on the nobility within your soul. Don't expect to get rich through a spouse—it's a shameful and disgraceful way to gain wealth. Don't seek to get rich in general. 'For the love of money is a root of all kinds of evil.' [1 Timothy 6:10] People who want to be rich fall into temptation, senseless and harmful desires, and end up in traps that lead to ruin and destruction. So, don't look for wealth from a a spouse; if you have that, everything else will come easily.

Who, tell me, neglecting what's most important, will care for lesser things? Yet, alas, this is our common mistake. Even when we have children, we don't focus on making them good people, but on finding them rich spouses. Not on how to make them well-behaved, but how to make them well-off. Even when we pursue a skill, it's not so we can be free from wrongdoings, but so we can gain a lot of money. Money has become everything. That's why everything has gone to ruin, because love for money has taken over us.

Men should love their wives as their own bodies, the text says. What does this mean? The example has evolved into a bigger and stronger image. But not just that, it has also become clearer and closer. "Look, there's a difference between a requirement and a gift. The first isn't really that necessary. So, let's say someone argues, 'Well, that was Jesus Christ, and he was God, and he gave himself up for us.' To counter that, it's like saying, 'This is what's owed.' It's not a gift; it's a debt. After mentioning how people should treat their own bodies, he added, 'No one ever hated their own flesh but nourishes and cherishes it.' [Ephesians 5:29] In other words, they take good care of it.

And how is the Church like Christ's body? Listen to this: He said, 'This is now bone of my bones and flesh of my flesh.' [Genesis 2:23] But not just that; he also said, 'They shall become one flesh.' [Genesis 2:24] Just like Christ loved the Church. He's the original example. Because we're parts of his body, made from his flesh and his bones. How? Because we're made from the same stuff, just like Eve was made from Adam's flesh. It's good that he mentioned both flesh and bones, as those are what make us up.

"Alright, so flesh and bones are like the most important parts of us, right? Think of the bones as the framework and the flesh as the building materials. It's pretty obvious over there, but what about over here? Just like there's a close connection in the physical body, the same goes for the Church. What does it mean that we're 'from his flesh'? It means we're genuinely part of him. And how are we parts of Christ's body? Because we're created in his image. And what about 'from his flesh'? Listen up, if you take part in spiritual rituals like Communion, that's how you're molded into being part of him.

How does that work? Well, listen to this: 'Since the children have flesh and blood, he too shared in their humanity.' [Hebrews 2:14] But notice, he joined us, not the other way around. So, how are we made from his flesh and bones? Some people say it's about the blood and the water from Communion, but that's not it. What he means is that just as he was born from the Holy Spirit without any physical relationship, we're also born in Baptism. Look at all these examples to make you believe in that special birth.

"Wow, these heretics sure don't get it! They're okay with saying that something born from water, like a baby, is a real being. But they won't accept that we become part of Christ's body. If we're not part of him, how does the phrase 'from his flesh and bones' make sense? Check this out: Adam was created, and Christ was born. Corruption entered the world through Adam's side, but life came through Christ's. Death sprang up in Paradise, but its undoing happened on the Cross.

So just like the Son of God is part of our human nature, we're part of his essence. Just as he has us within him, we also have him within us. This is why a person will leave their parents and unite with their spouse, and the two become one flesh. Here's a third point: it shows that someone will leave their parents, the ones they came from, and connect with their spouse. From then on, the flesh that comes from both—the parent and the child—is a mixture. When their 'seeds' mix, a child is born, so that "The three become one flesh.

In the same way, we become one with Christ through sharing. And it's even more the case for us than for a child. Why? Because it's been that way from the beginning. Don't tell me, 'It's like this or like that.' Don't you see that even in our physical bodies we have many imperfections? One person may limp, another may have crooked feet, another dry hands, and another some other weak part of the body. Yet, we don't suffer or cut these parts off. We often even prefer them because they're part of us. So, the amount of love each of us has for ourselves, we should have for our spouse.

It's not just that we share the same nature; it goes beyond that in our relationship with our spouse. Because we're no longer two bodies but one, with one being the head and the other the body. And how does it say elsewhere that the head of Christ is God? I say the same, that just as, "We are one body, just like Christ and the Father are one. So the Father is also our head.

There are two examples given: one of the body and one of Christ. That's why it's said: 'This is a great mystery; I'm talking about Christ and the Church.' [Ephesians 5:32] What does this mean? It says it's a great mystery because something amazing and wonderful is being hinted at, first by the blessed Moses but more so by God. Anyway, it says it's about Christ because he left his Father to come to his bride, and they became one spirit. 'Whoever is joined to the Lord is one spirit.' [1 Corinthians 6:17] And rightly so, it's called a great mystery. It's as if to say, 'But the allegory doesn't negate the love.' Each of you, individually, should love his own wife as much as he loves himself; and the wife should respect her husband.

It truly, truly is a mystery, and a great one, to leave the one who gave birth to you, who raised you, who went through the pain and trouble for you, the people who did so much good for you, the people you grew up with. "He attaches himself to her even though he's never seen her before and has nothing in common with her, choosing her above everyone else. It really is a mystery. And when all this happens, the parents aren't bothered by it. In fact, they'd be more bothered if it didn't happen. And they're happy even when money is being spent and costs are incurred. It's truly a great mystery, holding some kind of unspoken wisdom.

Moses foretold this from long ago, and Paul is shouting it now, saying it's about Christ and the Church. But this isn't just said for him, it's also for the wife, so that he might cherish her as his own flesh, just like Christ does the Church. And the wife should respect her husband. It's not just about love anymore, but also that the wife should respect her husband. The wife is a secondary beginning. So, she shouldn't demand equality; she is under the head. And he shouldn't look down on her as if she's inferior; she is his body. If the head looks down on the body, it too will suffer.

Instead, let love be the balance to obedience. Just like the head and the body; the one provides the hands, the feet, and the rest for service. "Every part of a relationship should be caring. One side looks out for the other, and both feel connected. There's nothing better than this partnership.

And how can love exist if there's fear, you might ask? Well, it can. The one who is afraid also loves, and the one who loves also feels fear but in a way that respects the other person. This creates a balance that brings peace. If everyone tried to be equal, peace would never happen. There must be one guiding force. And this is true in any relationship where people aren't spiritually mature. When people are spiritually mature, peace comes naturally. Five thousand people lived this way, and none of them considered what they had as solely their own; they all shared with one another. "This is what it means to be wise and to respect each other.

So, the way of love has been shown, but the way of fear hasn't been expanded upon. Why? Because love is more important to focus on. When there is love, everything falls into place. "Everything else follows when there's love, but not necessarily when there's only fear. Let's say a guy loves his girlfriend; even if she's not super easy to get along with, he'll still put up with a lot because he loves her. It's hard to have a solid relationship without the kind of love that really binds you together. Fear alone can't achieve that. So, love is focused on more because it's stronger.

A woman might think it's unfair that she's supposed to fear her partner, but he's actually been given the tougher job: to love. So, what if the woman doesn't feel fear? The answer is simple: you love, and you'll be fine. Even if other people don't follow along, you still should. It's like the saying, 'Submit to one another out of reverence for Christ.' [Ephesians 5:21] So what if the other person doesn't do their part? You should still follow God's rules. The same goes here: even if a woman isn't loved, she should still have reverence, so nothing falls apart.

"Even if a woman doesn't fear her husband, he should still love her, so he doesn't fall short; each person has their own role to play. This is what a marriage based on Christ's teachings is like—a spiritual union and a spiritual birth, not just physical. Take the marriage of Isaac and Sarah in the Bible as an example; Sarah was past the age of having children, so their relationship wasn't just physical, but deeply spiritual. When two souls come together in this way, only God fully understands it.

That's why it's said, 'Whoever is united with the Lord is one with Him in spirit.' [1 Corinthians 6:17] Notice how the focus is on uniting both body and spirit. So where are the people who say that marriage is a bad thing? If marriage were truly bad, why would Christ refer to it as a union of bride and bridegroom? He even quoted the saying, 'A man will leave his father and mother,' to emphasise that this unity is in Christ.

"It's also said about the Church. For example, the Psalmist says, 'Listen, daughter, and see; tilt your ear, forget your people and your father's house; and the king will desire your beauty.' [Psalm 45:10-11] This is why Christ also said, 'I came from the Father and have come here.' [John 16:28] But when I say he left the Father, don't think of it like people moving from place to place. Just as he is said to have 'gone out,' not because he left, but because of taking on a human body, similarly, 'He left the Father.'

So why didn't he also say about the wife, 'She will be united with her husband'? Why? Because he was talking about love, and he was speaking to the man. When he talks about fear, he says, 'The man is the head of the woman,' [Ephesians 5:23] and again, 'Christ is the head of the Church.' [Ephesians 5:23] When it comes to love, he talks to him, and gives him the responsibility for it, urging him to be committed and united.

For someone who leaves his father for his wife, and then leaves her again, how could he be worthy of forgiveness? Don't you see how much honour God wants her to have, that after taking you away from your father, he has attached you to her? So what if we do our part, but she doesn't follow? "If the unbeliever separates, let them separate. A brother is not enslaved." [1 Corinthians 7:15] The Psalmist talks about the Church, saying: "Listen, daughter, see, and bend your ear; forget your people and your father's house; the king will desire your beauty." [Psalm 45:10-11] Jesus also said: "I came from the Father and have come."

[John 16:28] But don't think He left the Father the way people move from place to place. It's different.

So, why didn't he also say that a woman will be united with her husband? Well, because he was talking about love and speaking to the man. When he talked about fear, he said: "The man is the head of the woman" [Ephesians 5:23] and "Christ is the head of the Church." [Ephesians 5:23] He gave the responsibilities of love to the man, binding him tightly to it.

If a guy leaves his dad for a girl and then leaves her too, what kind of forgiveness could he expect? Don't you see how much honour God wants her to have by binding you to her instead of your father? And what if things don't go as planned? If an unbeliever wants to separate, let them. "Brothers and sisters aren't bound in such cases." [1 Corinthians 7:15] But when you hear about fear, expect the free kind of fear, not like that from a slave. Your body is yours. Disrespecting it is disrespecting yourself.

So, what's this fear about? It means not to argue, not to rebel, and not to be bossy. Love will go beyond fear. It's a weaker gender, needing lots of help and understanding. What about those who remarry? I'm not saying this as a criticism, heaven forbid; even the Apostle allowed it. Be extremely understanding; provide everything for her, do everything for her, even if it's a hassle. You have to.

Here, there's no need to take advice from external examples, as is often done. The example of Christ is big and strong enough, even for the subject of submission. "'He will leave his father and mother,'" it says. [Genesis 2:24] Look, this is key: The text doesn't just say "they will live together." It says "they will be joined," emphasising a really tight connection. This suggests a love that's super intense.

But it doesn't stop there; it goes on to show a level of commitment that's so deep, the two don't even seem like two separate people anymore. It doesn't say "one spirit" or "one soul." Because that would be obvious, and anyone could do that. But this is saying that they become like one flesh, one body. This is a whole new level of closeness.

And there's more: even though both people in this relationship are super important, the man has something extra. This extra thing is really what saves the relationship. He not only needs to love, but he also needs to set the rhythm, to guide. The text says, "so that she may be holy and without blemish." [Ephesians 5:27] Both the "one flesh" part and the "they will be joined" part point to love as the central theme. "If you make her (the wife) holy and faultless, everything else will follow.

Seek the things of God, and human matters will come easily. Guide the woman, and in doing so, the household will be in order. Listen to what Paul says: 'If they want to learn something, let them ask their own husbands at home.'" [1 Corinthians 14:35] If we manage our households this way, we'll be ready to lead the Church; for the household is like a small Church.

In this way, by becoming good men and women, we will excel in everything. Consider Abraham, Sarah, Isaac, and the 318 servants in the household: see how the entire household was organised, how it was filled with reverence. Sarah also fulfilled the apostolic command, and she feared her husband; listen to her saying, 'I have never had a child, and my husband is older.'

"He loved her so much that he followed everything she advised. Their child was virtuous, and even the servants were amazing. They didn't hesitate to risk their lives for their master and didn't question him. One servant who was in charge was so exceptional that he was trusted with the marriage of the only child and also with tasks beyond their land. Just like in an army, when the soldiers are well-organised, no enemy dares to attack; in the same way, when husband, wife, children, and servants all take good care of the same things, there's great harmony in the household.

Because if that's not the case, often one bad servant can mess everything up and ruin it, and sometimes one person can destroy it all. So let's take great care of our wives, children, and servants, knowing that this will make our leadership easier for us, and we'll have gentle and fair responsibilities. And we can proudly say, 'Look, here are me and the children that God has given me.' [Isaiah 8:18] If the husband is admirable, and the head is good, then the rest of the body won't experience any trouble. So, about how a woman should behave well toward her husband, he said it very precisely: she should fear him as her head, and he should love her as his wife."

First Text: He loved her so much that he listened to whatever she asked him to do. Their child was truly wonderful, and so were the people who lived with them—so devoted to their master that they'd face any danger, without questioning why. One of them was especially trusted, even with arranging the marriage of their only child and handling things when they had to travel far away.

It's like in an army: When the soldiers are organised, enemies won't dare attack. Same here—when a husband, wife, kids, and everyone in the house are all looking out for each other, there's a lot of harmony. But if just one person messes up, it can wreck everything.

So we should take care of our wives, kids, and workers. If the head of the house is great, the rest will follow suit. A wife should respect her husband as her head, and the husband should love his wife.

Second Text: How can all this happen? Well, we need to not focus on money, aim for virtues of the soul, and always keep the fear of God before us. Whatever good or bad each one does, they'll receive from the Lord. "So, love her not just for her sake, but for Christ's sake. That's enough to bring about and convince people of peace, without leaving room for grudges or discord.

Don't let anyone sow discord between a husband and

wife. But neither should a husband be too quick to suspect his wife, nor should a wife be overly curious about his comings and goings. What good is it to spend the whole day with your friends and only the evening with your wife? Even then, you can't fully reassure her or keep her from being suspicious.

If your wife has complaints, don't get upset—it's out of love, not spite. It's the kind of love that yearns for better."

She was anxious and fearful. She was scared that someone might steal her bed, that someone might deprive her of her valuable possessions, or even take her life. She was always on the edge, suspicious that her servants might act against her, that her husband might conspire against her, and so on. These fears can even generate suspicion.

Think about the story of Sarah in the Bible. She herself told her husband, Abraham, to take Hagar as a second wife. She initiated this; nobody forced her. Her husband, Abraham, who had spent a long time without having children, chose to never become a father if it meant upsetting his wife. But what does Sarah say later? "Let God be the judge between you and me." [Genesis 16:5] Wouldn't someone else have gotten angry, maybe even yelled: "What are you saying? I didn't want to get involved with another woman; you started all this, and now you blame me?" But Abraham didn't react that way. Instead, he said, "Look, your servant is in your hands. Do with her as you please." [Genesis 16:6] He gave up his right to be with Hagar so as not to upset Sarah.

And yet, sharing one's life—that's what being married means—is the greatest act of trust. If even sharing a meal can create a bond, as the Psalmist says, becoming 'one flesh' in marriage should bind people even more strongly. Despite all this, Abraham gave in to his wife, showing that it wasn't his fault; he was merely trying to keep the peace. "He sent her away while she was pregnant. Who wouldn't feel sorry for a woman carrying a child from him? But the just man wasn't affected; above all, he prioritised love for his wife.

Let's follow this example: no one should shame their neighbour for being poor, no one should lust after wealth, and then everything will be fine. A wife shouldn't say to her husband: 'You're spineless and cowardly, full of laziness and sleep. Some guy, born humble and from humble beginnings, took risks and went abroad, and now he's rich. His wife wears gold and rides in a chariot pulled by white mules, she goes everywhere, has a household full of servants and eunuchs; but you've failed and live aimlessly.' A woman shouldn't say these things or anything like them. The body isn't meant to order the head around, but to obey and listen.

'How will he endure poverty? Where will he find comfort?' she might wonder. Let her think about those who are even poorer, consider how many noble daughters from noble families not only didn't receive anything from their husbands but also gave and spent all they had. She should think about the dangers that come from such wealth and will appreciate a life free from complications."

"And honestly, if a wife really loves her husband, she won't say stuff like that. She'd prefer having him as her partner even if he can't provide much, over a man who has tons of gold but is always stressed because he's constantly away on business trips. But also, hearing all this, the husband shouldn't let it go to his head and become abusive or resort to hitting. Instead, he should advise and counsel his wife, gently persuading her when she's being unreasonable. He should never raise his hand against her; that's far from the spirit of a free soul. So no abuse, no insults, no harsh words. Rather, he should guide her as someone less understanding."

"What will make this happen? If one understands true wealth and higher philosophy, they won't complain about such things. Teach them that poverty is not evil. Teach them not only through words but also through actions. Teach them to disregard fame, and then the woman will neither speak nor desire such things."

Just like you would welcome a statue into your home, teach her from the very evening she enters your bedroom. Teach her virtues like moderation and kindness, so she can lead a dignified life. Teach her to cast away the love for material wealth right from the doorstep. Educate her in philosophy and advise her not to wear gold hanging from her ears, cheeks, and neck, nor to have expensive, golden clothing lying around the room. Let the home be cheerful, but let the cheerfulness not cross into arrogance. Leave the ostentation for the stage and let your house be adorned with much modesty, smelling more of virtue than of any other fragrance.

Two things will happen from this, and three are beautiful: Firstly, the bride won't feel sad when the gifts and trinkets and silverware are sent away. "Secondly, the groom won't worry about losing or protecting the stuff they've gathered. Thirdly, and most importantly, this lifestyle will show everyone what he truly values. It will make clear that he takes no pleasure in material things and that he will dissolve all else that doesn't align with these values. He'll never allow for senseless dances or inappropriate songs.

I know some people might find these ideas laughable, but trust me, as time goes by and you experience the benefits firsthand, you'll understand the gain. The laughter will fade, and you'll laugh at how you used to live. You'll see that today's lifestyle is like that of clueless kids or drunken adults. What I'm suggesting is a life of wisdom, moderation, and the highest form of citizenship.

So, what am I saying you should do? Get rid of all the shameful songs, the satanic tunes, and the inappropriate lyrics. Stop hanging out with reckless young people. Doing these things will help your bride become more prudent. She'll immediately think to herself, 'Wow! What kind of man is this? He's a philosopher.'

"He doesn't care for the present life; he brought me into his home for child-rearing and household management. Will the bride find all this boring? Maybe for the first or second day, but not afterward. In fact, she'll find great joy in it, freeing herself from all sorts of suspicions. Because a man who can't stand flutes, dancing, or silly songs even at his wedding probably won't ever do or say anything shameful.

After you've gotten rid of all these elements from the wedding, and she joins you, shape her character well. Stretch out the initial period of awkwardness; don't rush through it. Even if the girl is not particularly shy, she'll still keep quiet for a while, out of respect for her husband and because everything is new to her. So don't quickly dissolve that initial awkwardness, like some men with no self-control do, but let it last for a longer time.

"Look, this will be a big win for you. She won't complain or find fault with whatever rules you set. So, make your rules during the time when she feels a sense of shame, when shame acts like a rein on her soul, keeping her from criticising or complaining. Because when she feels free to speak her mind, she can disrupt everything. So, when is the best time to influence her? When she respects you and is still a little afraid and shy. That's when you set all the rules, and she'll definitely listen, whether she wants to or not.

How do you keep that sense of shame alive? Show that you too feel shame, talk minimally, but meaningfully.

Then, introduce her to philosophy; her soul will welcome it. Guide her towards the best possible state, one of honourable shame.

And if you're wondering what you should talk to her about, I can give you some examples. If even Paul wasn't shy to say, 'Do not deprive one another,' [1 Corinthians 7:5] and spoke words not just about marriage but about the spiritual soul, then we should not hesitate to speak. So, what should you talk to her about?

"Speak to her with a lot of kindness and say, 'We chose you, my love, to share our lives with, and we're bringing you into the most precious and essential parts of our world—like raising kids and taking care of the home. So, what are we asking of you? Actually, before that, let's talk about love. Nothing convinces someone to listen to what you're saying more than knowing it comes from a place of love. How can you show this love? Well, if you say, 'I had many opportunities to be with people who were wealthier, more convenient, or from a well-known family, but I chose you because of your character, your decency, your kindness, and your self-control,' she'll be more inclined to listen to you. Then, you can smoothly transition into discussions about philosophy and even lightly criticise the pursuit of wealth. If you go on and on just criticising wealth, it's going to get annoying. But if you start with love as your foundation, your words will reach her heart. It'll seem like a natural progression of the conversation.'

"I'm not trying to be all serious and uncool here,

but listen. I chose you, not just because it was easy or convenient. I could have married someone rich, but I didn't. Why? Because I learned that wealth isn't really valuable; it's easy to lose and it attracts all the wrong people—like thieves and bad folks. That's why I turned away from all that and chose you for your inner goodness, which I value way more than any amount of gold. You're smart, free-spirited, and you actually care about being a good person, which is priceless in my eyes. That's why I love you and place you above everything else in my life. Life is short, you know? I pray and hope and do everything I can so we can live this life in a way that will let us be together in the next life with total freedom and peace. This time we have now is fleeting; if we live it right and make God happy, then we'll earn an even better life later on."

"Believe this: we'll always be together, both with Christ and with each other, experiencing even greater joy. Your love is the most important thing to me. Nothing is harder or more burdensome than the thought of being separated from you. Even if I have to lose everything, become poorer than ever, face the most dangerous situations, or endure anything at all, I'm willing to bear it as long as everything is okay between us. I will cherish our kids just as long as you remain good to us. But you need to act this way too. Then, remember the words from the Apostles: this is how God wants our goodwill to be formed. Listen to what the Scripture says: 'For this reason, a man will leave his father and mother and be united to his wife.' [Genesis 2:24] Let's not make excuses to be timid; let riches, large numbers of servants, and outside honours go away. All of this is less important to me than you. How much gold, how many treasures could be more cherished than these words to a woman? Don't fear that love will somehow fade; instead, openly declare your love. Some people flit from partner to partner and might get a kick out of hearing such words, but a free woman, a noble daughter, would never be inflated by these words; instead, she would be even more humbled. Show how much you value being together."

"Preferring to be at home rather than at the marketplace, he values his family above all friends. He cherishes his children and loves his spouse. If his spouse does something good, he praises and admires her."

If she does something questionable, like any young person might, he gently advises and reminds her. He speaks against excessive spending and extravagance, highlighting the beauty of modesty and dignity. He continuously teaches what's beneficial. May both of you share blessings; each should lead the way to church and engage with what is said and read there. A husband should look after the household, and so should the wife. If poverty is an issue, consider the holy men like Paul and Peter, who were more successful than even kings and the rich, despite their hardships.

Teach her that there's nothing in life to fear except offending God. If you marry in this manner, you'll be no less noble than those who choose to live alone or those who haven't married. If you wish to host dinners, avoid inviting disrespectful or rude people. Instead, if you find a holy, poor person capable of blessing your home, capable of bringing God's blessings with just the step of a foot into your home, invite them.

"Invite this person into your life. Can I offer another piece of advice? Don't rush to marry someone wealthier, but rather consider someone less fortunate. Money doesn't bring as much happiness as the resentment and quarrels it can cause—like demanding more than what was initially contributed, being arrogant, living extravagantly, or saying burdensome things. Your partner might say, 'I haven't spent any of your money yet; I still have what my parents gave me.' What are you saying? You still have your own assets? What does that even mean?

"What could be more tragic? You no longer have a body of your own after marriage, yet you still claim your wealth as your own? You're no longer two separate beings; you've become one. Yet your property remains divided? Oh, the love of money! You've become a single entity, a single life, and yet you still say, 'This is mine?' This awful mindset is a wicked invention from the devil himself. God has made the essentials common to us all—light, sun, water. So why aren't our belongings shared? May money perish a thousand times over! Or better yet, not the money, but the attitudes that don't know how to use money wisely and instead put it above everything else. Teach this alongside other virtues, but with a lot of grace.

Because virtue can often come across as stern, especially to a young and gentle girl hearing about philosophy, so use a lot of grace. Get rid of the idea of 'mine' and 'yours' from her mind. If she says, 'This is mine,' tell her, "What are you saying is 'yours'? I don't even know because I don't have anything that's just 'mine.' So how can you say 'mine' when everything is yours? Be kind with your words. Don't you see how we treat little kids? If they snatch something we're holding and then want something else too, we let them have it and say, 'Yes, this is yours, and that too.' Do the same with your spouse; her mindset is childlike. If she says 'mine,' respond with, 'Everything is yours, and I am yours.' This isn't flattery; it's true understanding. This way, you can calm her anger and extinguish her dissatisfaction.

Flattery is when you do something shameful for the sake of evil; this is high-level wisdom. So, say 'I am yours, my dear.' This is what Paul advised, saying, 'The husband does not have authority over his own body but yields it to his wife.' [1 Corinthians 7:4] If I don't even have control over my own body but you do, then even more so over our possessions. By saying these things, you'll calm her, extinguish the fire, shame the devil, make her more obedient, and bind her with these words. So, teach her to never say 'Mine' and 'Yours.' And never just call her plainly, but with flattery, with honour, with much love. Honour her, and she won't need honour from others; she won't need glory from others if she enjoys it from you.

"Put her above all else, for all reasons—her beauty,

her intelligence, and praise her for it. This way, you'll convince her to pay no attention to anyone else from the outside world, but to laugh at all others. Teach her the fear of God, and everything will flow like from a spring, and your home will be filled with countless blessings. If we seek the things that last forever, then temporary things will come our way too. For it is said, 'Seek first the kingdom of God, and all these things will be added to you.' [Matthew 6:33] Can you imagine what kind of children such parents would have? Or what kind of servants such masters would have? Or anyone else who comes close to them? Wouldn't they too be filled with countless blessings?

"Many are influenced by those in power, and slaves conform their morals to theirs, imitating their desires. They love what they are taught, speak the same words, and associate with the same people. If we discipline ourselves in this way and pay attention to the Scriptures, we will be better educated than many of them. In this manner, we will please God and live our entire lives with virtue. We will also obtain the promised blessings for those who love Him. May we all be deemed worthy of these, by the grace and philanthropy of our Lord Jesus Christ, together with the Father and the Holy Spirit, now and forever, and unto the ages of ages. Amen."

Chapter 4

THE DIVINE DUTY OF CHRISTIAN PARENTING

St John Chrysostom
Homily 21 (Ephesians 6:1-4)

"Kids, always listen to your parents because it's the right thing to do. Honour your mom and dad; this is a really important rule that promises you good things and a long life on earth."
(Ephesians 6:1-3)

Think about it like this: When someone is making a sculpture of a body, they start with the head, then the neck, and then the feet. In the same way, Paul, who was a really wise person, talked about things. He talked about men, then about women, and now it's about kids. A man leads his wife, but both the man and the woman lead their children."

"So, what does this mean? Kids, again, listen to your parents. This rule is really important. Here, Paul isn't talking about really big spiritual stuff or Christ. He's addressing simple, basic thoughts, which is why he keeps it short and simple. He keeps his advice short because he knows that kids might have trouble following a long discussion. That's why he doesn't talk about things like kingdoms; those topics aren't really meant for young ears. Instead, he talks about things that a young mind would want to hear, like living a long life."

"If someone asked, 'Why isn't he talking about kingdoms?', we'd say it's because he's addressing a younger audience. He knows that with the roles of men and women set in the way they are, it's not too hard to guide children. When you start something with a strong foundation, everything else follows easily. The hard part is setting up that foundation."

"He says, 'Kids, listen to your parents in the Lord's way', which means to listen as the Lord would want you to. 'He says that this is how God commanded. But what if parents ask their children to do something wrong? Well, usually a parent would never ask their child to do something harmful, even if they themselves are a bit off track. But just in case, it's clarified by saying 'in the Lord.' This means to follow their commands as long as they don't go against what God would want."

"So if a parent is pushing something that doesn't align with faith, like if they follow different beliefs or are misguided, then you don't have to obey. Because that's not really 'in the Lord.' He mentions this as being the 'first commandment,' but isn't it usually something like 'Don't cheat' or 'Don't kill'? He's not talking about the order of the commandments but rather the promise it holds."

"The other commandments are about avoiding wrongdoings, but honouring parents has a reward because it's about doing something good. Notice how wonderfully he places respect and honour for parents as the foundation of a virtuous path. Moving away from bad actions and aiming to do good things, the first thing emphasised is to honour your parents. After all, even before any other considerations in life, it's because of them, after God, that we're alive. It makes sense then that they should be the first to enjoy our good deeds, and then everyone else. If someone doesn't have this respect for their parents, they likely won't be considerate to outsiders either."

"After giving this advice to children, the focus shifts to parents. It says, 'Fathers, do not provoke your children to anger, but bring them up in the discipline and instruction of the Lord.' (Ephesians 6:4) It doesn't just say, 'Love them.' Because nature naturally draws parents to love their children and it would be redundant to set a rule about something so innate. Instead, it warns against aggravating your children, as many do, treating them like they're disowned, or burdening them too heavily, not as free individuals but as slaves. This is why it says, 'Do not provoke your children.'

"Then it gets to the main point, showing how children would naturally obey if they are treated with respect and kindness, pointing to the foundational cause of it all. Just as it was shown that the woman should listen to the man (and so he speaks more to him, urging her to be drawn by the powerful force of love), in the same way, the responsibility is brought back to him, saying, 'But raise them (the children) in the discipline and instruction of the Lord.' Do you see how spiritual matters are tied with physical ones? Do you want your son to be obedient? From the beginning, bring him up in the teachings and guidance of the Lord."

"Don't think it's unnecessary for him to hear from the sacred Scriptures. There, he will first hear, 'Honour your father and mother.' (Ephesians 6:2) This is beneficial for you. Don't say, 'This is only for those who live in solitude; for I don't make him live in solitude.' He doesn't necessarily have to live that way. Why are you afraid of losing a lot? Make him a Christian. Especially for those living in worldly matters, it's essential to know these teachings, especially for the children. Young age can be quite thoughtless, and this lack of judgement is even increased by external influences."

"When they learn from their surroundings about heroes who are actually slaves to their emotions and are afraid of death, like Achilles when he regrets, when he dies for a concubine, when another becomes drunk, and many other such stories, he then needs antidotes for these poisons. Isn't it strange to send them for art and to schools, doing everything for this purpose, but not to raise them in the Lord's teachings and guidance?"

"Kids, do you know why we often enjoy the first of the fruits? It's because we sometimes raise our children to be bold, unruly, disobedient, and lacking discipline. But we shouldn't do this. Instead, we should listen to wise advice: raise them with discipline and the guidance of the Lord. Let's set an example for them, introducing them to the writings of Scripture from an early age."

"I know some of you might think I'm just rambling on, but I won't stop sharing this important message. Why don't you follow the examples of the people from ancient times? Especially you, young women, admire and emulate the great women of the past. Remember when a child was born to Anna? She immediately took him to the temple. Wouldn't any of you want your son to be like Samuel, rather than just a worldly king?" (1 Samuel 1:24-28)

"And you might ask, 'How can my child become like that?' It's possible if you desire it and entrust him to those who can guide him that way. And who can do that? God can. Anna entrusted her son to God. Eli, the priest, wasn't perfect, as even he couldn't guide his own sons. But Anna's faith and determination made the difference. Anna first gave birth to Samuel and she didn't even know if she'd have other kids. She didn't say, 'Let me wait for him to grow a bit, to get involved in everyday matters or enjoy his childhood.' Instead, her primary concern was how to offer her child, her spiritual treasure, to God from the very beginning."

"Men, we should learn from the dedication and philosophy of this woman. She offered her child to God and left him there. That's why her marriage and life flourished. She prioritised spiritual matters, and after offering Samuel to God, she was blessed with more children and saw success in the world. If people honour those who honour them, wouldn't God do much more, even without expecting honour in return?"

"Why are we so focused on the physical? Why do we keep our sights so grounded on the earth? We should prioritise the care of our children and raise them with discipline and the Lord's guidance."

"If a child learns the value of wisdom from an early age, they gain a wealth greater than any material riches and a reputation more powerful than fame. Teaching them a trade or skill to earn money isn't as valuable as teaching them the art of valuing inner wealth over material wealth. If you want to make your child rich, teach them this way. True wealth isn't about having lots of possessions, but about not needing anything at all. Educate your child in this mindset. This is true wealth. Don't just aim for your child to succeed in external knowledge and gain worldly reputation. Instead, teach them to value inner worth over fleeting fame. This perspective will make them shine brighter."

"Both the rich and the poor can adopt this mindset, learned not from teachers or crafts, but from sacred teachings. Don't just wish for your child to live a long life on Earth; aim for them to have an everlasting life beyond. Give them the bigger picture, not just the small details. Listen to what Paul says: 'Raise them with the Lord's guidance. With guidance and teachings from the Lord, don't push him to become a skilled speaker, but rather educate him in philosophy. For without the former, there will be no harm, but without the latter, all the eloquence in the world won't bring any true gain. We need good character, not just words; virtue, not just skill; actions, not just statements. These principles pave the way to leadership and grant genuine goodness. Don't just sharpen the tongue, cleanse the soul.'" (Ephesians 6:4)

"I'm not saying don't teach these things; I'm saying don't focus only on them. Don't think that only monks need this education from the Scriptures. Especially those entering this world need it. Just as someone who's always at the harbour doesn't need knowledge of shipbuilding, navigation, or a crew as much as someone who's always sailing does, so it is with worldly and monastic lives. One lives a calm life, like a still harbour, free from every storm, while the other is always at sea, battling frequent storms. Even if he doesn't need it for himself, he should be prepared to guide others. So, the more successful he becomes in life, the more he needs this education."

"If he lives among royalty, many Greeks, philosophers, and those celebrated for their current reputation, will surround him, like a place filled with water. Royalty is like this: everyone is puffed up and inflamed; even those who aren't royal aspire to be. Imagine then, your son entering such a realm. He's like a top-notch doctor who comes with tools capable of calming each person's inflammation. He approaches each person, conversing and healing their ailing bodies, applying remedies from the Scriptures, and sharing wisdom from philosophy."

"Who does a monk converse with? The walls and the ceiling? The wilderness or the trees and birds? A monk may not have a great need for such teachings, yet he still strives to perfect them, not so much to teach others, but to improve himself. Those living in this world especially need such teachings. If you wish to understand, he'll be even more effective in the real world. Everyone will respect him for his words, especially when they see he remains untouched by desires, like standing in fire without burning, or not craving power. In fact, he might even gain power when he doesn't seek it, and he'll become more respected than a king. Such a person can't be overlooked. Among many healthy people, one healthy person goes unnoticed, but among many ill, one healthy person stands out. News of his well-being will quickly spread even to royal ears, capturing the attention of many. Knowing this, raise your children in the Lord's education and guidance."

"But what if he's poor? Being poor again? Yet, one turning to royalty will be no less esteemed. Not being in royal courts, he'll be admired and quickly recognized. Philosophy will come by choice, not by appointment. If certain Greeks, who are superficial and act like dogs, adopt a shallow philosophy (because that's how Greek philosophy is sometimes), or rather just the name of philosophy, and go around with long hair and rough clothes, they upset many people. How much more then will the truly wise philosopher do? If a false image, a mere shadow of philosophy, can attract so much attention, what if we love genuine and pure philosophy? Won't everyone admire and respect it? Wouldn't they entrust their homes, wives, and children to such people?"

"But there's no true philosopher like that now. That's why it's hard to find a good example. Some are in monasteries, but in ordinary life? Not really. Although there are some in monasteries, I'll mention one from many. You probably know and some of you have seen him: the wonderful Julian. He was a simple man from humble beginnings. He wasn't educated in worldly matters but was full of pure philosophy. Whenever he entered a city (which was rare), people gathered around him like no other orator, sophist, or anyone else could gather. What am I saying? Isn't his name still brighter than all kings?"

"If this is the case in our world, where we were promised no good thing by our Master, and where we're told we are strangers, imagine the rewards waiting for us in heaven! If they were strangers there and still received such honour, how much more will they enjoy in the heavenly cities? If hardships were promised here but they received so much care, how relaxed will it be where real honours are promised?"

"But do you want examples from everyday life? We don't have any right now. Maybe there are decent everyday folks, but they haven't reached the pinnacle of philosophy. So, I'll tell you about the old, holy examples. There were many who had wives and raised children, and they didn't lack any of the things mentioned before. But now, there's no one like that because of the current necessities, as the blessed man says."

"So, who do you want me to talk about? Noah? Abraham? Abraham's son or Noah's? Or should it be Joseph? Do you want us to move on to the prophets? I'm talking about Moses and Isaiah. But let's focus on Abraham, as everyone always brings him up. Didn't he have a wife? Didn't he have children?" (Genesis 17:19, Genesis 21:2-3)

"I'm saying this to you as you often point out to us. He had a wife, but that's not what made him amazing. He had wealth, but having wealth isn't why God favoured him. He had children, but just because he had children doesn't mean he was blessed. He had 318 servants, but that's not why he was admired. So, why then? It was because of his hospitality, his humility despite his wealth, and his decency."

"What does it mean to be a philosopher? Isn't it about looking beyond wealth and fame? Rising above jealousy and every other emotion? Let's bring Abraham into focus and analyse him, and I'll show you what kind of philosopher he was. He wasn't overly attached to his homeland. When he heard the call 'Leave your country and your family,' he immediately left." (Genesis 12:1)

"He wasn't overly attached to his house. For he did not go out for no reason; not because of the usual friendships, not for any other thing or person. Above all, he despised fame and wealth. Even when he won a war and was entitled to the spoils, he rejected them. But his son admired him not because of the wealth, but because of his hospitality; not because of the servants, but because of his obedience; not because of the woman, but because of his self-control concerning her. They didn't value the life they lived in the present, they didn't seek wealth, they looked beyond all that."

"Tell me, which plant is the best? Isn't it the one that gets its strength from home, and is not harmed by rain, hail, wind gusts, or any such irregularity, but stands bare, looking down on all, needing neither barriers nor walls? This is what a philosopher is like, this is that kind of wealth: he has nothing, and yet he has everything; he possesses all, yet holds nothing. For the wall is not inside, but outside; the barrier isn't natural, but something added on."

"Tell me, what body is strong? Isn't it the one that is healthy, and doesn't fall victim to hunger, overeating, cold, or heat? Or the one always exposed to these and depending on carpenters, weavers, hunters, and doctors to stay healthy? The true rich person is the real philosopher, the one who needs none of these things. This is why the blessed one said, 'Raise them with the discipline and instruction of the Lord.'" (Ephesians 6:4)

"So, don't wrap barriers around you from the outside; for this is wealth, this is honour. For when these things fall away, and they will, the plant stands bare and vulnerable, having not only gained nothing in the past but also having been harmed. Those protective barriers that prevent it from exercising against the assaults of the wind, it has now made them fall altogether. So, wealth often does more harm, making us unprepared for life's challenges. Let's raise our children in such a way that they can withstand anything and aren't surprised by what's coming. Let's nurture them in the teachings and guidance of the Lord, and a great reward will await us."

"If people get so much honour from making statues of kings and painting their portraits, won't we gain a multitude of blessings for enhancing the royal image of God (for humans are in God's image) by giving it its true resemblance? This resemblance is the virtue of the soul, when we educate our children to be good, not to hold grudges, to be forgiving. All these traits are God-like, when we teach them to be charitable, loving towards all, and not to value material things over everything else. This should be our mission: to shape ourselves and them rightly. How can we stand confidently before Christ's judgement seat otherwise?"

"If someone is considered unfit for leadership because they can't manage their own kids, then how much more for the kingdom of heaven? Will we be held responsible if we have an unruly spouse or children? Yes, if we don't diligently address our own responsibilities. Our own virtue is not enough for salvation."

"If someone who didn't invest even one talent and gained nothing is punished, it's clear that personal virtue alone won't save us, but also the virtue of another." (Matthew 25:29-30)

"So, let's care deeply for our wives, pay great attention to our children, and also to our servants, and especially ourselves. We ask God to guide us and be with us in our tasks. If He sees us genuinely trying and putting in effort, He will assist us. But if we don't care or put in any effort, He won't lend a hand. God doesn't just help those who sit around doing nothing; He helps those who also help themselves. A helper is not there for someone who does nothing but for someone who is actively working."

"However, the good Lord has the power to complete the task on His own. We pray that all of us may receive the blessings promised, through the grace and love of our Lord Jesus Christ. Together with Him, the Father, and the Holy Spirit, be glory, power, and honour, now and forever, for ages to come. Amen."

Scan the QR code to go to our

website where you will find

Book reviews

Great deals

Our full library of books

www.ingramcontent.com/pod-product-compliance
Lightning Source LLC
Chambersburg PA
CBHW031201160426
43193CB00008B/464